To my twin boys, the double scoops of joy in my life's sundae – this flavorful collection is my gift to you.
To my sister, whose brilliant idea sparked this culinary adventure.
To Mom, who taught me to transform simple ingredients into magic.
To my husband, the brave taste tester of every kitchen experiment.
And to all who've seasoned our days with laughter and love.
Each recipe here captures a shared moment, simmered in joy.
Ready, set, giggle and bon appétit!

the aroma of spices,
a melody in the air,
whispers of magic and culinary flair
Turn the page, and let our flavorful journey commence.

vibrant

refreshing

succulent

comforting

nostalgic

flavortastic

wonders

contents

butterfly pea lemonade

ingredients

perfect for 4 food lovers

- Butterfly Pea Flowers (dried) - 1 to 2 tablespoons (10-15 flowers)
- Hot Water - 1 cup (for steeping the butterfly pea flowers).
- Freshly squeezed Lemon Juice -1/2 cup
- Cold Water - 2 cups
- Sugar or Honey - 2 to 4 tablespoons (according to taste).
- Ice Cubes - as needed.

Optional Garnishes:
- Lemon slices
- Sage or mint leaves

directions

20 mins flavor journey

- Steep the dried butterfly pea flowers in 1 cup of hot water for 5-10 minutes until the water turns deep blue.
- Strain out the flowers and let the tea cool.
- Add 2 cups of cold water and sweeten with sugar or honey to taste. Stir well until the sugar or honey dissolves.
- In a pitcher, mix the butterfly pea tea with the lemon juice. Watch as the color changes to purple.
- For those who want to spike it up add 1/2 cup vodka, gin, or white rum (adjust to your preference)
- Fill glasses with ice cubes and pour the lemonade over the ice.
- Garnish with lemon slices and sage leaves if desired.
- Serve immediately and enjoy your refreshing butterfly pea lemonade!

glamming it Up !

Sense and Sensibility - The magical color change adds oomph! Balance acidity with butterfly pea tea for vibrant hues. A little lemon turns purple; more lemon gives it a bright pink. Experiment with lime or orange for subtle variations.

magical midsummer night dream

I never thought I'd find magic in my own kitchen, but there I was, feeling like a modern day Puck from my beloved play "A Midsummer Night's Dream". It all started when I stumbled upon curious little butterfly pods at a local brunch place. Their deep blue color reminded me of the enchanted forest we'd created for our high school play years ago.

On a whim, I decided to brew them into a lemonade. As I poured the steaming blue liquid into a pitcher, I couldn't help but grin - it was as if I'd captured a piece of the summer sky. But the real magic happened when I added the lemon juice.

I gasped as the blue transformed before my eyes, shifting to a vibrant purple, then a delicate pink. It was like watching the chaotic love story of the Athenian youth unfold in my glass! Each color change felt like a plot twist, a new act in this little flavor play I was creating. Tasting it was another revelation. The tangy lemon danced with the subtle, earthy notes of the butterfly pea, creating a flavor as complex and refreshing as Shakespeare's verses. With each sip, I was transported back to those carefree days of high school theater, of painted cardboard trees and glitter dusted fairy wings.

Now, whenever I'm in the mood for some magical time, I love to serve this alluring concoction. The wide eyed wonder as people watch the colors shift never fails to delight me. It's become my signature potion, a way to sprinkle a little enchantment into our everyday lives.

Who knew that a simple lemonade could become such a storyteller? Cool, refreshing, with a twist of whimsy that would make even stern Oberon crack a smile.So, how about we raise a glass to this colorful adventure.. quench our thirst, and, perhaps, add a splash of enchantment to an ordinary day? After all, as Lysander says, "The course of true love never did run smooth" - but I promise you, this lemonade certainly does!

refreshing peach delight

ingredients

perfect for 4 food lovers

Cocktail

4 ripe peach slices
1/2 ounce fresh juice from 1 lemon
1/2 ounce rosemary simple syrup (see recipe below)
1 1/2 ounces bourbon (optional)

Rosemary Simple Syrup:
1 cup sugar
1 cup water
1 sprig rosemary

directions

30 mins flavor journey

The Syrup

Combine water, rosemary, and sugar in a small saucepan. Boil over high heat, stirring to dissolve sugar. Reduce to a simmer and continue to cook for 10 minutes. Remove from heat and let it cool. Strain through a fine mesh strainer.

The Drink

Start by blending peaches, ice, and simple syrup until smooth. For added flavor in a cocktail shaker, muddle a few peach slices with rosemary syrup to release their flavors. Then, add the blended peach mixture to the shaker, along with lemon juice and bourbon. Shake the contents vigorously for 10 seconds to combine and chill the ingredients. Carefully strain the cocktail through a mini strainer into a cocktail glass to ensure a smooth texture. Finally, garnish the drink with a fresh rosemary sprig.

g **lamming it Up !**

Garnish Glory: Transform your cocktail into a stylish ensemble with eye-catching additions. From earthy rosemary to vibrant citrus twists, elegant fruit skewers to delicate edible flowers - each garnish carries its own tasteful statement!

juicy state of mind

In California, peaches hang like golden orbs of promise, their fuzzy skins whispering tales of sun soaked orchards and forgotten dreams. As July unfolds, announcing the peak of peach season, I find myself swept up in a fruity frenzy that still catches me by surprise years after moving here.

At the farmers' market, I weave through the crowd like a botanist on a mission. My fingers dance over fuzzy skins - the peach vendor, his face as weathered and warm as a well loved book, offers a knowing smile. "The usual?" he asks, and I nod, feeling like I've been inducted into some secret summer society.

Back home, our kitchen transforms into a scientist's lab. My husband is amused, eyebrows raised, as I attack our backyard rosemary with the focus of a surgeon. "Don't worry," I assure him - "I'm not crazy just inspired!"

Did you know peaches and roses are botanical cousins? This little fact makes me feel like a horticultural genius as I muddle ingredients with a mixologist's flair. As the blender whirs, I can't help but think of my first California summer - my life here, like this concoction, is about blending the familiar with the unexpected, the sweet with the complex.

That first sip captures a California sunset in a glass. Peach sweetness tangoes with piney rosemary, an unlikely but perfect pairing. In this peach crazed state, I feel connected to a rich history of cultivation, from John Augustus Sutter's 1841 orchards to Sutter County becoming the "Peach Bowl of the World" in the 1960s.

As I savor my peach rosemary creation, I'm tasting more than a drink - I'm sipping California's legacy. Here, even the wildest mix of ideas and experiences finds its harmony. Who knew that moving west would turn me into a fruit obsessed alchemist? But in the land of golden dreams and fuzzy possibilities, stranger things have blossomed!

khaman bites

ingredients

perfect for 4 food lovers

1.5 cups besan (chickpeas flour)

1 tablespoon sooji (semolina)

1 cup water (240 ml)

2 tablespoons sugar

1 teaspoon salt

1.5 teaspoon ginger-chili paste

1/4 teaspoon turmeric

1.5 tablespoons oil

3/4 teaspoon citric acid (lemon juice)

1/4 teaspoon baking soda

1 teaspoon plain ENO

Tempering

2 tsp black and white sesame seeds

1.5 tsp mustard seeds

1 tsp oil

directions

40 mins flavor journey

The Batter

Sift: Combine 1 cup besan and 2 tbsp sooji.

Mix Wet Ingredients: Mix 1 cup water, 2 tbsp sugar, salt, ginger-green chili paste, turmeric, 1.5 tbsp oil, and citric acid (lemon juice).

Combine: Add sifted ingredients to the wet mixture. Adjust water for a thick but pourable batter.

Rest: Cover and let sit for 10 minutes.

Prepare Steamer: Boil 2.5-3 cups water and grease the steaming pan.

Leaven: Mix 1 tsp baking soda or ENO into the batter.

The Tempering

Heat Oil: Heat 2 tsp oil, add mustard seeds.

Spices: Add curry leaves, and sliced green chili. Stir.

Cool: Let dhokla sit for 5-10 minutes.

Unmold: Use the Cookie cutter to cut into cute shapes and top it with the tempering and some chutney.

Healthy Twist - you can make them even healthier with an oats or quinoa twist if you're feeling adventurous. Enjoy!

glamming it Up !

Delectable Sculpting - let's get a bit fancy with the presentation. Cookie cutters are your best friends think floral shapes like tulips or classic squares and circles. Top it all off with some green chutney, harissa, or thick tomato chutney. A tadka of mustard and sesame seeds, and a sprinkle of herbs like thyme, mint, or cilantro - adds that final touch. Voila, your Dhokla is ready to dazzle with a hint of French flair.

spilling the be(san)

In the maze of my culinary memories, there's a yellow path paved with squares of spongy delight. It leads not to Oz, but to Gujarat, where the humble dhokla reigns supreme in the court of appetizers.

At parties, where chatter rises and falls like waves, appetizers are the mischievous show stealers. They play on tongues, telling stories of far off kitchens. Among these world-traveling bites, my heart belongs to a simple yellow square - the Dhokla, a fluffy emissary from Gujarat.

Now picture old Greeks munching on early snacks, their togas sprinkled with crumbs. Then came the French, who with a shrug, named these nibbles "hors d'oeuvres" and made them trendy. But darlings let's turn to our real star: the "Dhokla Delight", a soft, puffy dream that's won Indian hearts with the tenacity of a particularly stubborn curry stain.

At parties, Dhokla is the king, second only to the samosa - that triangle troublemaker. Old Indian wisdom says Dhokla is good for you, like a warm hug for your insides on a cold day. Who knew healthy could taste so much like tangy, fermented goodness?

Now, lean into this juicy bit of Guju food gossip. A riddle wrapped in a mystery, covered in chickpea flour: Is Khaman really Dhokla? Oh, the heated debates this has sparked! Imagine a bunch of Gujaratis, armed with spatulas and strong opinions, arguing the finer points of fermentation. Khaman and Khatta Dhokla, you see, are food cousins. One's made from chickpeas, the other from rice and lentils.

So, my dear friends, next time you find yourself at a soirée, armed with this nugget of knowledge, do enlighten the masses. Watch as eyes widen and jaws drop at your dhokla discourse. For in the end, whether Khaman or Dhokla, isn't it all just deliciously, gloriously delicious?

roasted cauliflower

ingredients

perfect for 4 food lovers

Main Dish
Whole cauliflower
Sea Salt
1 TBSP of Olive oil

The dressing
2 tbsp Zaatar
1 tbsp of rose Harissa
1 cup 2% plain Greek yogurt
1/4 cup Basil
1/4 cup Mint
1/2 Lemon juiced
4-5 cloves of garlic pressed.
2 tbsp Olive Oil
Pinch of salt and black pepper

directions

80 mins flavor journey

Step 1
Blanch a medium sized cauliflower, either whole or cut into florets. For picky eaters or those less fond of cauliflower, add a few potatoes and bell peppers to the mix for extra appeal.

Step 2
Drizzle the cauliflower (and any added veggies) with olive oil, a squeeze of lemon, and a sprinkle of salt. For florets, roast at 500F for 20 minutes. For a whole cauliflower, roast it in an oven covered with aluminum foil at 400F for 30 minutes, then uncover and continue roasting for another 35 minutes.

Step 3
While the veggies are roasting, blend za'atar, rose harissa, yogurt, basil, mint, and optional capers into a zesty paste. Once the veggies are done, drizzle the paste over them. For extra spice and vibrancy, substitute rose harissa. Top with cracked pepper or sunflower seeds for added flavor, and enjoy your delicious, crowd-pleasing dish!

glamming it up !

Color Theory: Why settle for basic when you can go bold? Elevate your dishes with a pop of color! Think vibrant purple cauliflower, radiant carrots, or pink potatoes. Not only will your taste buds thank you, but your plate will be serving up serious style points too.

autumn variations

Ah, autumn! The season of cozy sweaters, crunchy leaves, and... cauliflower? I know what you're thinking: "Cauliflower? Really?" But hear me out! This humble veggie is the Meryl Streep of the produce aisle it can play any role you throw at it!

I'm at the farmers' market, surrounded by pumpkins and carrots then, I spot the unassuming cauliflower next to it some pizzazz of its vibrant hues. Let me pause and share a quick fact – Cauliflower traces its roots back to ancient Cyprus. Thats right! This Mediterranean gem was cultivated long before it became a dinner table star.

What hooked me on cauliflower was its secret identity as a color maestro. Forget boring white!

How about an orange so vibrant it could outshine a traffic cone? Or a purple so deep it whispers secrets of the universe? And let's not forget Romanesco it's like Mother Nature showing off her geometry skills!

In my kitchen, cauliflower is a versatile artist. One day it's pretending to be pizza crust, the next it's masquerading as wings at a party. On chilly nights, it transforms into a comforting aloo gobi that warms you from the inside out.

And let's talk about health benefits. This cruciferous wonder is packing more nutrients than a superhero convention. It's got antioxidants, fiber, vitamins you name it!

So next time you're at the grocery store or farmers market, give that cauliflower a second glance. It might just become your new autumn fling. Who needs a pumpkin spice latte when you can have a cauliflower steak sizzling on your stove?

Now, if you'll excuse me, I'm off for some Cauliflower Appreciation Day!

kosambari quinoa salad

ingredients

perfect for 6-8 food lovers

3/4 cup cooked quinoa

1 cup diced cucumber

1/2 cup cherry tomatoes, halved

1 cup cooked black-eyed beans

1 cup drained and soaked dal yellow moong

1/2 cup grated carrot

1/2 diced jalapeno (optional)

1/4 cup chopped cilantro

1/4 cup chopped mint leaves

2 tablespoons lemon juice

1/2 teaspoon black pepper

1/2 teaspoon toasted cumin

Salt to taste

1 cup mixed salad leaves

1/4 cup shredded fresh or thawed frozen coconut

1/4 cup peanuts

1 tablespoon chia seeds

directions

25 mins flavor journey

Combine the cooked quinoa, cucumber, boiled black eyed beans, drained soaked dal, tomatoes, shallot, diced jalapeno (optional), cilantro, and mint leaves in a medium mixing bowl.

Add the lemon juice, black pepper, toasted cumin powder, and salt. Mix well and adjust the seasoning to taste.

Gently fold the salad leaves and garnish with shredded fresh coconut, peanuts, cherry tomatoes, and a dash of everything bagel seasoning or tadka of mustard seeds.

Chill the salad in the refrigerator for 1 hour before serving.

Enjoy your refreshing and nutritious salad!

glamming it Up !

Earthen Elegance: We've covered garnishes and color theory, so let's talk serving styles! For an earthy vibe, use a terracotta dish it's like giving your kosambari a cozy home! If you're out of luck, any glass or metal dish works too. Just remember this salad shines brightest when served chilled!

dressed to impress

always loved salads - one healthy habit I'm so proud of! Growing up salad was a simple affair - a medley of cucumber, onion, carrot, and tomato, and over time salad has taken me on a whirlwind culinary adventure.

Especially moving to the US, I discovered salads with more personality or mystery than a spy novel. Burmese tea leaf salad, anyone? Or the beetroot salad with an exotic punch to it! And I must have done something right as my boys have inherited my leafy love! We simply are in love with salads!!

But let's take a step back - the term "salad" originates from the Latin word "sal," meaning "salt. The Romans and Greeks first introduced the concept of mixing greens with salt, vinegar, and oil, creating the foundation for the modern salad. Fast forward salads began to be adorned with various herbs, flowers, and spices. - masterpieces of culinary art.

The true magic, however, lies in the dressings a harmonious blend of oil, acid, emulsifier (honey or mustard), and seasoning that transforms a bowl of greens into a symphony of taste.

In my quest to make my vegetarian salad protein packed, I've created my twist on the South Indian side dish kosambari. It's tropical, fresh, and packed with protein. Classic Kosambari, Kosumalli, or Koshambari is typically made from pulses, and cucumber, and seasoned with mustard seeds. My version has all of that but also quinoa and a protein packed black eyed twist to it and instead of the tadka, I prefer the garnish of fresh coconut, cilantro, and lemon juice with a dash of everything bagel seasoning or chia seeds.

So here's to salad - dressed to impress! May your leaves always be crisp and your dressing always bursting with flavor.

polenta bites

ingredients

perfect for 6-8 food lovers

The rounds
1 tube of pre-cooked polenta
2 tablespoons olive oil
Salt and pepper to taste

The toppings
tomato
arugula
white navy beans (cooked or can)r

directions

25 mins flavor journey

Preheat your oven to 450F (232C) (Or you can use the Air Fryer)
Slice the polenta into 3/4-inch thick rounds.
Brush both sides of the polenta rounds with olive oil and season with salt and pepper.
Place the rounds on a baking sheet lined with parchment paper or coated with cooking spray.
Bake for about 10 minutes on each side until golden brown and crispy.

Toppings
A mix of chopped fresh tomatoes, basil, and arugula with white beans for protein, drizzled with a balsamic reduction

or

Mushrooms and Caramelized Onions:
Sautéed mushrooms combined with caramelized onions create a rich, umami flavor that pairs well with the mild taste of polenta

glamming it Up !

The Drizzle: Elevate your dish with a balsamic reduction drizzle. This simple technique adds a rich, tangy flavor and creates an elegant visual contrast. Use a squeeze bottle to create delicate patterns or swirls on light-colored dishes. Remember, less is more a little drizzle goes a long way in both taste and presentation.

much ado about something

Who knew that a humble corn mush could cause such a stir in my culinary world? Polenta, once a stranger on my plate, has become the unexpected entry in my kitchen dramas. Like a Shakespearean comedy of errors, my journey with this golden grain has been filled with misunderstandings, revelations, and ultimately, a delicious resolution.

Polenta and I? I gave it the cold shoulder for years, barely acknowledging it on menus. We were strangers, not even close to dreaming of each other. Yet here I am, writing an ode to this golden ground corn, proving that love can bloom in the most unexpected kitchen corners. My children, with their adventurous palates - adore it. My friends - utterly bewitched. Serve it to someone who's never tried it, and you'll see more confusion than someone trying to solve a Rubik's cube for the first time. "What is this mysterious yellow thing...hmmm... potato?" they wonder.

For me, It all began on a camping trip, when we accidentally ordered polenta cake at a restaurant on our way home. One bite and it was a revelation! This humble corn dish, once the sustenance of peasants in Northern Italy, suddenly shone in a new light.

Polenta's journey from peasant fare to culinary star is nothing short of remarkable. Originally made from chestnut flour before corn arrived from the Americas, it has been a staple in Italian cuisine for centuries. Now, it's the darling of fancy restaurants and home kitchens alike.

When I need a crowd pleaser for my Italian theme dinner, I go back to my camping epiphany. I whip up some polenta bites, perfect for my vegan friends and easy to cook. As I wait for it to set, I muse, 'Polenta's like a good relationship - starts a bit mushy, but with patience and the right heat, it turns into something amazing. Now, I'm in love with polenta. It's the little black dress of my kitchen - versatile, reliable, and always chic. I'll pair it with ratatouille for French flair or make my own 'Del Contadino' - a nod to its rustic roots. With that excuse me dear friends I have a date with this golden delight and a hot oven. Ciao!

gnocchi saag

ingredients

perfect for 2-4 food lovers

Gnocchi
1 Tbsp unsalted butter, 1 Tbsp extra-virgin olive oil
12 oz/340 g homemade or store-bought gnocchi

Saag (Sauce)
1/2 lb/230 g fresh or frozen baby spinach
1/4 cup/60 ml + 1 Tbsp water
1 shallot or small white or yellow onion
2 garlic cloves, 1 tsp grated ginger
1 tsp kasoori methi
2 Tbsp plain unsweetened Greek yogurt
1 tsp ghee, melted unsalted butter, or vegetable oil
1 tsp homemade or store-bought garam masala, 1/4 tsp ground cayenne
fine sea salt

Tadka (Seasoning)
1 tbsp ghee or unsalted butter or olive oil
1 tsp whole cumin, sesame seeds
1 whole red chilly ,1 tsp ground coriander
3 to 4 tbsp crumbled paneer or goat cheese or cream, for garnish

directions

40 mins flavor journey

Gnocchi
Brown butter in skillet, add oil. Pan-fry gnocchi until crisp.

Saag
Cook spinach with 1 Tbsp water in covered skillet, medium heat, 8-10 mins until wilted. Stir occasionally. Transfer to blender. and add shallot/onion , garlic, ginger, kasoori methi, and 1/4 cup/60 ml water, and blend until smooth.
Heat the oil/ghee, add garam masala and cayenne, and stir with a spatula until the spices turn fragrant, 30 to 45 seconds. Fold in the spinach purée and Greek yogurt -Taste and season with salt. Transfer to a serving bowl. Fold in the cooked gnocchi.

Tadka
Sizzle cumin seeds in hot ghee, then quickly add minced garlic, one deseeded green/red chili, and a pinch of hing, frying until the garlic turns golden and fragrant, optionally tossing in a few curry leaves at the end for an extra aromatic punch.

glamming it up !

Tadka the firecracker - bring your dish to life with a burst of color and texture! - the golden sheen and vibrant hues make your gnocchi not just delicious but a feast for the eyes. It's not just about taste tadka elevates your food's presentation so much that you'll be itching to dig in!

james beard's passage to india

Ever feel like your kitchen has turned into a chore factory - so mundane and boring? Yeah, me too. But don't worry I'm here to share my secret weapon against cooking fatigue - the culinary crushes!

It all started with the classics. Julia Child's butter loving antics and Ottolenghi's veggie wizardry kept my cooking mojo alive. But little did I know, a new obsession was about to take over: the James Beard brigade.

The idea sparked during a trip to New Mexico, where I experienced flavors that set my taste buds dancing. The mastermind behind this culinary revelation? Katherine Kagel, a James Beard winner. That moment marked the birth of my James Beard Expedition ritual.

For those who may not know, the James Beard Award is as coveted in the food world as the Oscars are in film. It's the ultimate recognition of culinary excellence.

* adapted from Nik Shamra's blog

Inspired by Beard's philosophy "I don't like gourmet cooking or 'this' cooking or 'that' cooking. I like good cooking" I ventured on an adventure. From swooning over pastries at Jinju Bakery in Portland (diet? What diet?) to hunting down Beard nominees in every new city, I felt like I had discovered a secret foodie treasure map.

This journey led me to my current flavor crush: Nik Sharma, a molecular biologist turned chef. His gnocchi saag is like the best of India and Italy on one plate, and I couldn't resist adding my signature "tadka" twist.

So, let's spice up our kitchen lives together! Grab your apron and remember: that cooking is about feeding your joy. Let's get cookin'!

sabudana yogurt parfait

ingredients

perfect for 4 food lovers

Masala Layer

1 tsp ginger, finely chopped

1 cup sprouted black chickpeas or moong

1 cup sweet potatoes, baked or fried

1/2 cup chopped onion, tomatoes and cucumber

1 tsp chaat masala, salt to taste

2 tbsp cilantro, finely chopped

Sabudana Layer

1 cup small sabudana peals (tapioca or sago)

2 tbsp oil

1 tsp cumin seeds

4 curry leaves

1 tsp black pepper

I cup peanuts, crushed coarsely

1 tbsp beetroot, grated

1 tbsp lemon juice

Yogurt Layer

1 cup yogurt, beaten

2 tbsp mint cilantro chutney

2 tbsp tamarind chutney

directions

40 mins flavor journey

Beetroot Sabudana Preparation:

Soak sabudana in just enough water to cover for 3-4 hours. Drain and dry on a towel. Heat oil in a pan, add cumin seeds, and curry leaves. Add sabudana, peanuts, black pepper, salt, beetroot, lemon juice, and cilantro. Cook until sabudana turns translucent (2-3 minutes). Cover and set aside.

Masala

Heat oil, sauté ginger, green chilies, and sprouted chickpeas or moong beans for 2-3 minutes. Add baked chopped sweet potatoes, spices, salt, and sauté for 4-5 minutes. Mix in lemon juice and cilantro.

Assembling the parfait

In a serving bowl, layer yogurt, top it with tamarind and mint chutney, then add masala, mint-cilantro chutney, veggies (cucumbers, onions, tomatoes), and tamarind chutney. Top with beetroot sabudana. Garnish with sev and cilantor and peanuts

glamming it Up !

Crystalline Canvas: Use clear glass or crystal parfait cups to showcase the beautiful layers of ingredients. These clear, beautiful glasses add a touch of elegance to your parfaits, making every bite feel like a glamorous treat!

life's creamy comfort

For me, yogurt is more than just a food - it's a creamy comfort that feels like home. The reliable friend who never cancels plans, always there to cool life's fiery curries. But it's more than just a comfort food - it's a protein packed powerhouse that dieticians swear by. With 10 to 23 grams of protein per serving, it's the perfect pre or post workout snack.

Speaking of perfect, let's talk parfaits. Life is, much like a well crafted yogurt parfait, all about layering the right ingredients. A dollop of wisdom here, a sprinkle of humor there, all coming together in delicious harmony. And just as life has its sweet and savory moments, so does yogurt.

Sweet parfaits loaded with fruits and honey? Absolutely! But don't shy away from the savory side, especially if you're on one of those sugar free kicks. Trust me, savory yogurt can be just as delightful.

Now, let me serve you a tasty bit of history. During the Mughal era, royal doctors prescribed yogurt to balance out spicy foods and counteract the alkaline waters of the Yamuna River. Who knew we owed our beloved yogurt filled chaat dishes to the banks of the Yamuna?

In Ayurveda, yogurt is considered sattvic food - nourishing the body, calming the mind, and delighting the taste buds. As some wise soul once said, -

* adapted from "maturally nidhi's" blog

"Life's too short to skip the yogurt or the laughter." So whether you're Team Sweet or Team Savory, grab a spoon and dive in. Your gut and of course your taste buds will thank you!

curried noodle

ingredients

perfect for 4 food lovers

For the Curry Base:

1 tbsp vegetable oil

1 tbsp Thai red curry paste or Tom Yum Soup paste (adjust to taste)

4 - 5 tbsp coconut milk

1 tbsp water

For the Noodles:

8 oz (225 g) rice noodles or your favorite noodles

1 cup mixed vegetables (bell peppers, onion, julienned zucchini, snap peas, etc.)

1 cup extra firm tofu, cubed (optional)

Fresh cilantro, for garnish

Lime wedges, for serving

Chopped peanuts or cashews, for garnish (optional)

directions

35 mins flavor journey

Cook the noodles according to the package instructions. Drain and set aside.

Prepare the Curry Base:

- In a large pan or wok, heat the vegetable oil over medium heat.

Add the Thai red curry paste or Massaman curry paste and sauté for 1-2 minutes until fragrant.

- Pour in the coconut milk and water, stirring to combine. Bring the mixture to a simmer and allow it to cook for about 5 minutes to reduce slightly.

- Add the mixed vegetables and tofu to the curry sauce. Cook for about 5-7 minutes until the vegetables are tender but still crisp, allowing any excess liquid to evaporate.

- Add the cooked noodles to the pan, tossing gently to combine and absorb the flavors. If the mixture seems too wet, let it cook for an additional 2-3 minutes to dry it out a bit, stirring occasionally.

-Divide the curried noodles into bowls. Garnish with fresh cilantro, black sesame, and a drop of sesame oil along with lime wedges, and chopped peanuts or cashews, if desired.

glamming it Up !

Crunchy Confetti: Add a colorful and crunchy topping by sprinkling crushed peanuts, toasted coconut flakes, and crispy fried shallots over your noodles. This adds texture and visual appeal.

curried away

In my house, basketball is life, and Steph Curry is the "Curry Factor" we can't stop talking about. But today, I'm dishing on a different kind of curry the one that's been setting taste buds on fire across the globe.

Growing up, curry was my Indian comfort blanket. But oh boy, did my world open when I realized curry isn't just an Indian thing it's like the quintessential dish of Asian cuisine, popping up everywhere from Thailand to Japan with its own local twists!

So, let's take a taste bud tingling tour of curryville, shall we?

First things first "curry" comes from the Tamil word "kari," meaning sauce. (Thanks, British

colonizers, for spreading that spicy goodness!) At its heart, curry is all about that spice blend – turmeric, cumin, and chili having a party in your mouth. Throw in some onions, garlic, and maybe coconut milk, and you have a curry base that'll make the best chef jealous.

Now, buckle up for a whirlwind curry tour! Indian curries? They're like a Bollywood movie dramatic, colorful, and guaranteed to leave you wanting more. Thai curries? Imagine lemongrass and galangal doing a fox trot in your bowl. Japanese curries? The new kids on the block – mild and sweet perfect for curry newbies. And Caribbean curries? They're the rebel child, mixing Indian spice with African flair.

A wise person once said, "Curry is like an adventure book for your mouth. Mild for the cautious, medium for the brave, and 'Holy mother of spice!' for the daredevils." So, grab a spoon, and get curried away!

punjabi kadhi

ingredients

perfect for 4-5 food lovers

Pakoras

1 cup Chickpeas flour (besan)

1 small onion (thinly chopped)

1 potato (thinly chopped)

1 tsp red chili powder

1/2 tsp caraway seeds (ajwain)

Salt to taste

Water (to make the batter)

Oil (for frying)

Curry Base

1 cup yogurt (room temp)

1/2 cup Chickpeas flour (besan)

1/2 tsp turmeric powder

1 tsp Kashmiri chili powder

A pinch of asafoetida (hing)

1/2 green chilies (optional)

Salt to taste

4 - 5 cups water

1 tsp fenugreek (methi) seeds

Tadka

-ginger garlic paste 1 tsp

1/2 small onion

- 1 medium tomato - puree /chopped

- 1/2 tsp mustard seeds

- 1/2 tsp cumin seeds

- dried fenugreek & cilantro leaves

- chili olive oil

directions

50 mins flavor journey

Pakoras:

Mix all dry ingredients in a bowl.
Gradually whisk in water to make a thick,
smooth batter.
Add chopped fenugreek leaves or spinach
leaves and mix well
Heat oil in a pan. Drop spoonfuls of batter
into the hot oil and fry until golden and
crispy. Drain and set aside.

Kadhi:

In a large bowl, whisk together yogurt,
besan, turmeric, red chili powder, and salt.
Gradually add water to make a smooth
mixture.
Pour the mixture into a pan, stirring
constantly to avoid lumps. Bring to a boil,
then simmer for 30-40 minutes, stirring
occasionally. (For a relaxed approach, use the
slow-cooking setting on an Instant Pot.)

Tadka (Tempering):

Heat oil or ghee in a pan, add cumin seeds,
mustard seeds, and asafoetida. Let them
splutter, then add dried red chilies.
Add chopped onions, green chilies, ginger-
garlic paste, and sauté until onions turn
golden. Stir in tomato paste or diced
tomatoes, then add fried fenugreek leaves.
Putting it all together : Add the pakoras just
before serving to keep them crispy..

glamming it up !

The Swirl Effect: Before serving, use a spoon to create a whimsical swirl in the kadhi for an
elegant touch. For extra flair, add a swirl of chili olive oil or ghee sprinkled with everything
bagel seasoning to elevate the presentation!

rooted in tradition

In the grand theater of my kitchen, where pots and pans play percussion to the sizzle of spices, the remarkable women of my family take center stage. My mother, armed with boundless 'maa ka pyar', transformed cooking into a delicious science experiment. She humored the chemistry student and budding cook in me with recipes as precise as chemistry formulas, always including that special ingredient: love. Through her letters, filled with verses and kitchen wisdom, she taught me that both cooking and life flourish with a dash of balance.

My sister, my original 'spice girl', brings our traditions to life with pizzaz. Her creations, from Chinese bhel to pani puri, are flavor bombs that make me fall for our culinary creativity all over again - a Shah Rukh whispering, 'Come, fall in love. Marriage expanded my galaxy, bringing more flavors to the mix. My sister-in-law, sweeter than Gulab Jamun, impresses with her kindness and cooking prowess, while my younger sister-in-law's simple approach reminds me that sometimes, less is more. And my mother-in-law? Her Punjabi classics, even something as 'basic' as halwa, are grand opus in their own right.

Speaking of Punjabi cuisine - here's a delicious plot twist. While Punjabi kadhi is famous worldwide, its origins trace back to Rajasthan's arid landscapes, where clever cooks used dairy to make up for scarce vegetables. It's a reminder that even our most beloved dishes carry surprising histories, just like our family stories.

These lovely women, my spice board, have seasoned my life with their grace, courage, and curiosity. To these pillars of my culinary world - may your cooking pots always be full, your stories always flavorful, and your lives always brimming with joy and success. After all, in the recipe of life, it's the people who truly bring out the flavor.

gulab jamun cheese cake

ingredients

perfect for 6-8 food lovers

Cheese Cake

2 tsp Lime or Lemon, zest

1/4 cup Lime juice

6 oz Baking chocolate, white

3/4 cup Sugar

32 Ladyfingers, soft

2 packages (8 ounces each) cream cheese

1 cup Heavy whipping cream, whipped

1 envelope Gelatin, unflavored

20-30 pistachios coarse grinded

1 tsp cardamom powder

Gulab Jamun

10-12 store-bought gulab jamuns

or GITS 3.5 oz gulab jamun packet with 20 mini gulab jamun. Sugar syrup is optional for the recipe for GITS or homemade.

directions

50 mins flavor journey

The Layers

Arrange ladyfingers around the edges and bottom of an ungreased 8-in. springform pan.

In a small saucepan, sprinkle gelatin over cold lime juice; let stand for 1 minute. Heat over low heat, stirring until gelatin is completely dissolved.

Meanwhile, beat cream cheese and sugar until smooth. Gradually beat in melted chocolate, lime zest, and gelatin mixture. Fold in whipped cream.

Assemble

Pour half the cream cheese mixture into the prepared pan. Arrange the halved or quartered gulab jamuns evenly over the mixture. Pour the remaining cream cheese mixture over the gulab jamuns, spreading it evenly.

Sprinkle with grounded pistachio and rose petals some sliced or whole jamuns

Cover and refrigerate until set, about 3 hours minimum.

glamming it Up !

Floral finesse: Want to give your desserts that extra 'ooh la la'? Sprinkle a confetti of dried rose or lavender petals on top. It's like adorning your sweet creation with nature's confetti, turning a simple dessert into an insta worthy masterpiece. This touch not only adds a pop of color but also infuses your treat with subtle floral notes, creating a multi-sensory experience.

kuch meetha ho jaye

Did you know that the average Indian consumes about 1.5 kg of sweets during Diwali week? That's enough sugar to fuel a small rocket or send a dentist into early retirement!

Diwali, ah Diwali! The festival that turns every Indian into a part-time maid and full-time sugar addict. Growing up, it was the ultimate trifecta: a break from studies (yay), house cleaning with the precision of a surgeon's scalpel (nay), and enough sweets (yay) to make a dentist weep with joy. The air is thick with cardamom and rosewater, courtesy of Kumar Sweets, the real MVPs of Dehradun's mithai scene. My sister would eye the gulab jamun like a cat eyeing a particularly plump mouse, while I'd be in a committed relationship with chumchum. Oh, the sweet, sticky nostalgia!

Fast forward to today. Diwali week is the same circus of lights, sounds, and sugar highs. There I am, feet swinging, nose twitching, wondering what classic dish to whip up. Suddenly, a wild recipe idea hits me like a rogue firecracker - why not bridge continents and generations in one delicious swoop? Gulab Jamun Cheesecake - the familiar scents of tradition mingled with the promise of something new, like wearing sneakers under your saree.

My son still reminisces about my fusion masterpieces, but this year, I need to up the ante. It's time to bring back the dish with some Diwali swag. Time to make some sweet magic happen - and perhaps contribute to that 1.5 kg average.

healthy fruit cake

ingredients

perfect for 10-12 food lovers

80g sorghum flour
60g almond flour
20g coconut flour
3 tablespoons chia seeds (+ 9 tablespoons water, set for 10 minutes)
Extra coconut flour (for dusting)
200g dates
100g dried figs
100g dried apricots
2 apples, grated
Juice from 2 oranges
60ml (1/4 cup) maple syrup
5 tablespoons coconut oil
60ml (1/4 cup) plant milk
1 tsp vanilla bean paste or extract
1 tsp ground cinnamon
1 tsp ground ginger
1 tsp ground nutmeg

directions

50 mins flavor journey

Preheat oven to 175C/350F. Grease and line a 20cm round cake tin with baking paper. Chop dried fruit into 1 cm pieces. Combine in a bowl with grated apples, orange juice, coconut oil, plant milk, vanilla, maple syrup, and chia gel. Set aside.

In a separate bowl, combine all flours and spices. Gradually add dry mixture to wet ingredients. Adjust consistency if needed - if too dry, add more plant milk; if too wet, add more flour.

Pour batter into prepared tin. Bake 1 to 2 hours, or until a toothpick inserted comes out clean.
Cool in tin for 20 minutes, then turn out onto cooling rack. Allow to cool completely.
Optional: dust with coconut flour before serving.

Sprinkle with grounded pistachio and rose petals some sliced or whole jamuns
Cover and refrigerate until set, about 3 hours minimum.

glamming it Up !

A Citrusy Affair: Top with delicate orange zest ribbons or candied citrus slices. For special occasions, pair with matching macarons (fig-honey, orange-almond, or spiced date) or crown with fresh fig quarters and a light honey drizzle. A dusting of gold-tinted coconut flour adds the final sparkle.

to royalty and beyond

What words dance through your mind when winter bells chime? Snow, cookies, Santa, and... a dessert that can survive a trip to space, outlast empires, and surprise you with a 106-year-old slice still lurking in New Jersey, looking about as appetizing as last year's Christmas leftovers!

Oh darling, yeh hai fruitcake - the dessert that refuses to die! In Manitou Springs, Colorado, these dense beauties soar through winter air like fruity comets during their annual Great Fruitcake Toss Day. Because sometimes, it's more fun to launch your food than to eat it!

But my memories are sweeter, thanks to Mrs. Daniel, my neighbor - bless her heart and her annual tradition. Every December, we'd await her masterpiece gleaming with glazed cherries like rubies in a very brown, very dense crown.

I always shied away from making one myself, thinking it was a Herculean task. For me, food should be a quick statement, not a long project - as spontaneous as my fashion choices: bold, immediate, and occasionally questionable!

* adapted from Teffy's sprinkle of greens

And here's a royal whisper: Queen Victoria waited an entire year to eat her birthday fruitcake. Imagine that patience! Now it's a royal family signature, gracing every wedding table like a fruity crown jewel - you're not truly royal until you've served this timeless treat.

Oh darling, yeh hai fruitcake - more enduring than a holiday hangover and packed with more ingredients than a medieval apothecary's cabinet. It's been to space, graced royal tables, and might outlive us all. But now? I'm sharing a healthy take that proves it's not so Herculean after all!

gathered here.....

spring into cuteness
pistachio cookies

power puffs
paneer tarts

wine pairings
herbed olives and nuts

gathered here for the oohs and the
aahs,
on a route where each flavor just soars.......

hello summer
watermelon peach salad

spanish sizzle
saucy potato bravas

power peals
panjeeri

......making moments all bright,
Every bite pure delight,
'where there's good food, good moods' by the
scores!

Welcome to my "Flavortastic Wonders," where words and flavors collide in a delicious explosion of creativity! This book is your ticket to fun culinary adventures, where kitchen experiments lead to happy surprises and every meal tells a story.

Cooking, for me, is like inviting you into my home - minus the awkward small talk and frantic tidying. It's about crafting experiences, turning simple ingredients into memories, and flavors into tales worth sharing. Whether you're a solo diner or feeding a crowd, you'll find honest chats and inspiration to make your taste buds dance.

Dive into fusion recipes born from late night cravings and dining experiences. Discover tips to transform cooking creations into culinary triumphs. And along the way, you'll get a glimpse into my flavorful journey.

So, grab your favorite spatula, fire up the stove, and let's whip up some joy together!

Warning: Side effects may include spontaneous cravings, impromptu cooking sprees, and a newfound appreciation for kitchen shenanigans. Best consumed with an empty stomach and a hearty appetite for adventure!

www.ingramcontent.com/pod-product-compliance
Lightning Source LLC
Chambersburg PA
CBHW041630110726
48005CB00002B/556